Be Careful Who You Trust!

Story by Graham Maxwell   Pictures by Kevin Harkey

Pineknoll

Publications
REDLANDS, CALIFORNIA

Text © 1996 by Graham Maxwell
Illustrations © 1996 by Pine Knoll Publications and Kevin Harkey

Published by Pine Knoll Publications, Redlands, California 92373 USA

Design: Kevin Harkey and Linda Wheeler
Typography/Composition: Linda Wheeler, Win Graphics

Library of Congress Cataloging-in-Publication Data

Maxwell, A. Graham (Arthur Graham), 1921 –
    Be careful who you trust! / story by Graham Maxwell : pictures by
Kevin Harkey.
        p.   cm.
    Summary: When he goes to deliver a message from God to Jeroboam,
a prophet from Judah sadly learns that not everyone, including
prophets, can be trusted.
    ISBN 1-56652-006-1 (alk. paper). – 1-56652-005-3 (pbk. :
alk. paper)
    1. Jeroboam I, King of Israel – Juvenile literature.   2. Prophets-
-Juvenile literature.   3. Bible stories, English – O.T. Kings, 1st.
[1. Jeroboam I, King of Israel.   2. Bible Stories – O.T.]
I. Harkey, Kevin, ill.   II. Title.
BS580.J44M38   1996
222'.5309505 – dc20   96-41279
                                                        CIP
                                                        AC

Wouldn't it be wonderful to live in a world where everyone could be trusted! But almost daily in the news we hear sad stories about people who have been too quick to trust.

The Bible tells the story of a prophet who made the serious mistake of believing someone who was not safe to trust. And the one who proved so untrustworthy was himself a prophet. You see, prophets too can lie! The mistake cost the unwise prophet his life.

The story begins in the days of Jeroboam, who became king after the death of famous King Solomon. Jeroboam was not a true believer in God. He even set up young bulls made of gold for the people to worship.

One of the places where King Jeroboam sacrificed to these idols was the city of Bethel.

God sent a stern warning to Jeroboam, and he asked a prophet from neighboring Judah to deliver the message. The prophet crossed the border and arrived in Bethel just as Jeroboam was standing at the altar ready to offer sacrifice.

"O altar, altar!" the prophet cried. "This is what the Lord says." And he went on to describe how Jeroboam's heathen altar would someday be used to stop the worship of false gods.

Then the prophet from Judah gave Jeroboam a sign to help the king take God's warning seriously.

"This altar will be torn down,
and the ashes on it will be scattered
on the ground. Then perhaps you will believe
that what the Lord has said will really come true."

When King Jeroboam heard
what the prophet said about his
altar, he pointed at him and shouted . . .

"Arrest that man!"

Suddenly the king's outstretched hand withered up
and he couldn't pull it back.
    Then the altar fell apart, and the ashes spilled out
on the ground — just as the prophet had said.

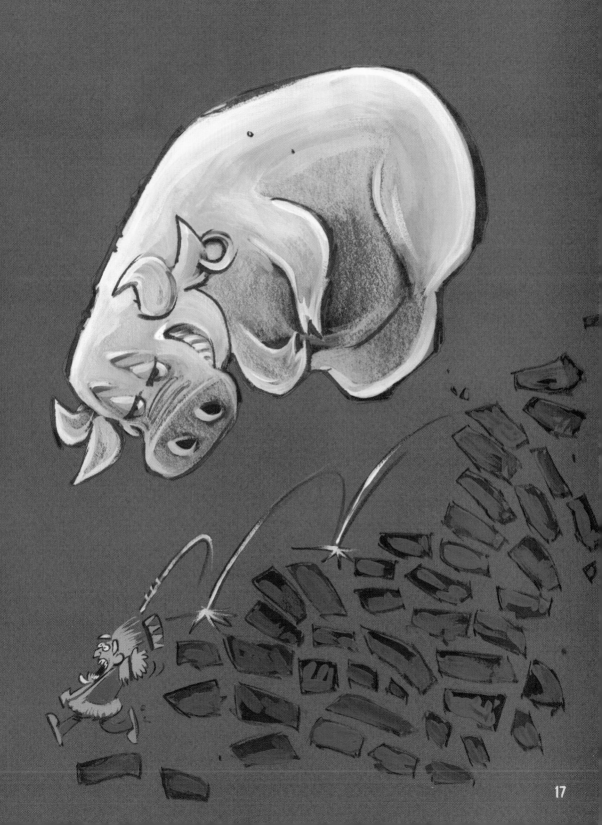

King Jeroboam begged the prophet, "Please pray to your God for me, and ask him to heal my hand."

So the prophet prayed to the Lord.

In answer to the prophet's prayer, the withered hand was healed. And to the king's great delight, it looked just as it did before.

Jeroboam was so pleased
to be healed that he gave
the prophet a royal
invitation.

"Come home with me and have something to eat.
And for all you've done I'll give you a present too."

"I cannot accept your invitation," the prophet replied. "Even if you gave me half of everything you have, I would not go with you. God told me that I am not to eat or drink anything in this place. I also must not go home the same way I came here to Bethel."

So the prophet obeyed what the Lord had commanded and left for Judah by a different road.

TAKE 13

At that time there was an old prophet living in Bethel. One of his sons came and told him what the prophet from Judah had done in Bethel that day and what he had said to the king.

"Which way did he go when he left?" the old prophet asked.

His sons showed him the road, and the old man
hurried off to catch up with the prophet from Judah.

When he finally found him he asked, "Are you the prophet who just spoke to the king?" "Yes I am," he replied.

"Then come home and have a meal with me,"
said the old prophet.

Without hesitation the prophet from Judah
replied, just as he had to the king, "I can't go home
with you, because the Lord clearly commanded me
not to. And I would not think of disobeying God."

"No problem!" said the old prophet. "You see, I too am a prophet, just like you. And God sent an angel to tell me that I should take you home with me to Bethel and offer you something to eat."
But the Bible says the old prophet was lying!

"Well, if God said it's all right, then of course I'll be glad to come," said the younger prophet. "I've always followed the old rule that if God says it, I believe it, and that settles it."

So the prophet from Judah went all the way back to the city of Bethel.

When they arrived at the lying prophet's house, they sat down at his table and began to eat and drink together.

But while the young prophet was still enjoying his food . . .

a frightening message came from God to the older man.

He passed the message on
to the prophet from Judah.

"The Lord says that you have disobeyed him.
And your disobedience is so serious it will cost
you your life."
But he didn't tell him how he would die.

After they had finished eating, the deceitful prophet helped the younger one get ready for his trip.

Then he watched him leave
with his donkey — back down the
road to his home in the land of Judah.

On the way a lion met the younger prophet and killed him. But he didn't eat the body. Nor did he attack the donkey.

For a long time the lion and the donkey just stayed there together right beside the body of the prophet from Judah.

You can read the rest of the sad story in the thirteenth chapter of the first book of Kings.

P.S. How the story could have ended . . .

"I appreciate your invitation," said the surprised prophet from Judah. "But first I must check back with God."

"In that case," the old prophet muttered,
"just forget the whole thing!"

You could raise many questions about this story.
And God always invites us to ask him, "Why?"

But there is one thing that seems very clear.

Be careful who you trust!

The Author

Graham Maxwell is emeritus professor of New Testament at Loma Linda University. He earned his Ph.D. in Biblical Studies, New Testament, from the University of Chicago Divinity School.

His publications include *You Can Trust the Bible, I Want to be Free, Can God be Trusted?*, and most recently, *Servants or Friends? Another Look at God.*

His favorite course has been a year-long trip through the whole Bible to discover the picture of God in each of the sixty-six books. He has taught this course at least 136 times, not only in the classroom, but in churches and homes, to people of all ages and in groups ranging from a dozen to 700.

Maxwell has watched the effect of such Bible study on over 10,000 people. "Something seems to happen," he says, "when people of all cultures discover in the Bible a consistent picture of God – an awesome but friendly Person they can really trust and admire."

One thing Maxwell especially admires about God is his willingness to meet people where they are and speak a language they can understand – even using a talking donkey in the Old Testament story of Balaam! From the services of the tabernacle at the foot of Mt. Sinai, through the incredible story Jesus told about the rich man and Lazarus, and on to the amazing scenes in the book of Revelation, God has painted dramatic and colorful pictures of the truth.

Artist Kevin Harkey understands this language very well and has used it with special skill in *Be Careful Who You Trust!*

The Artist

Kevin Harkey has been working in feature animation for 15 years. Some of his projects have included story artist on Disney's *Beauty and the Beast, Aladdin, Lion King* and *Hunchback of Notre Dame.* He is currently working on Disney's *Tarzan.*

Kevin lives in southern California with his artist wife and two children.